MW01627490

This book is dedicated to the best teachers I've ever had—my children. May you follow your hearts, hold your heads high, and continue to spread your light wherever you go. Mama loves you.

www.mascotbooks.com

WHAT COLOR IS MY PATKA?

For more information, please contact:
Mascot Books
620 Herndon Parkway, Suite 320
Herndon, VA 20170
info@mascotbooks.com

Library of Congress Control Number: 2020922991

CPSIA Code: PRT1220A
ISBN-13: 978-1-64543-647-8

Printed in the United States

WHAT COLOR IS MY PATKA?

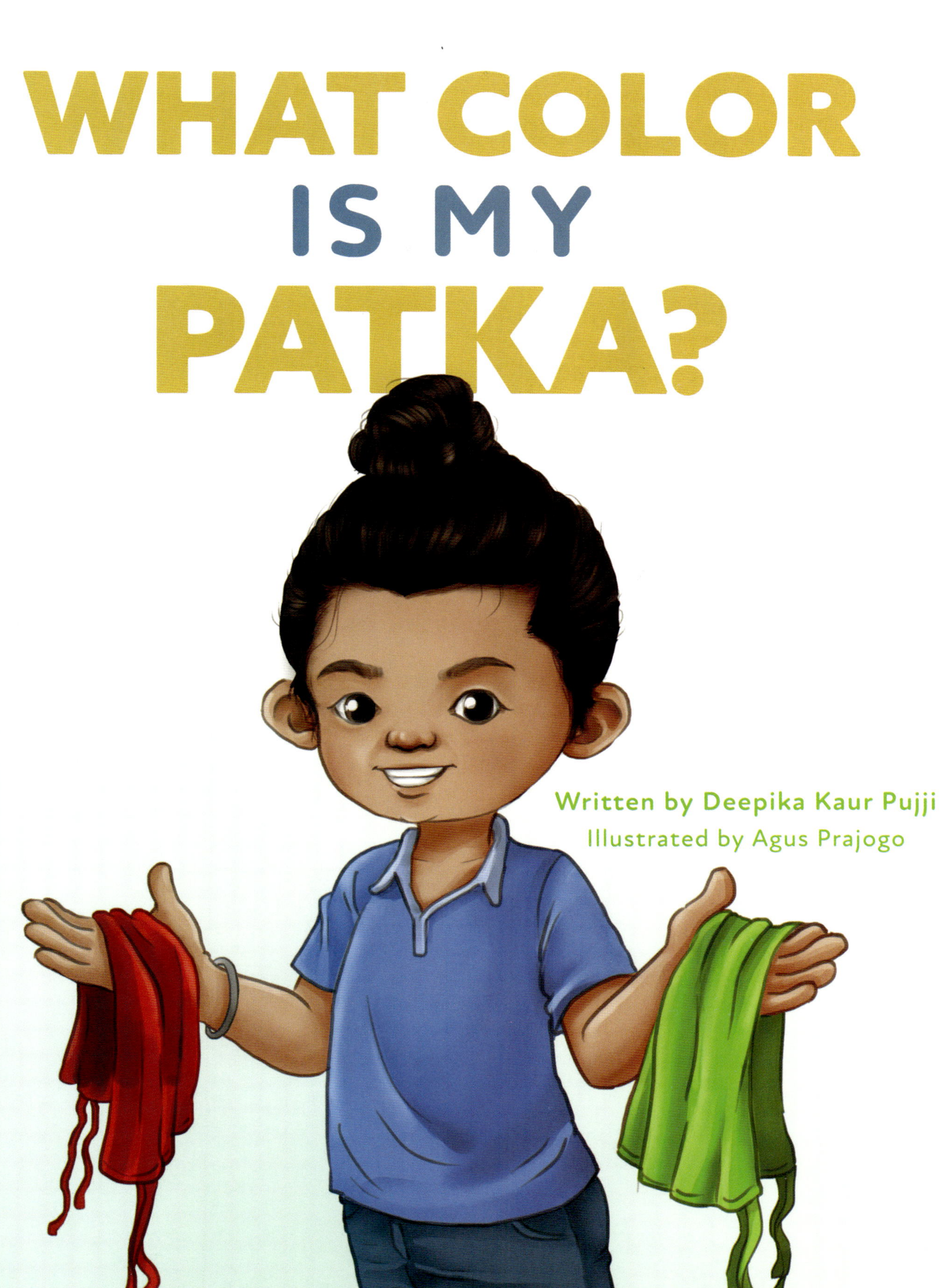

Written by Deepika Kaur Pujji
Illustrated by Agus Prajogo

Hello! I'm Ricky! I am a Sikh.
Today, will you help me choose which color patka to pick?

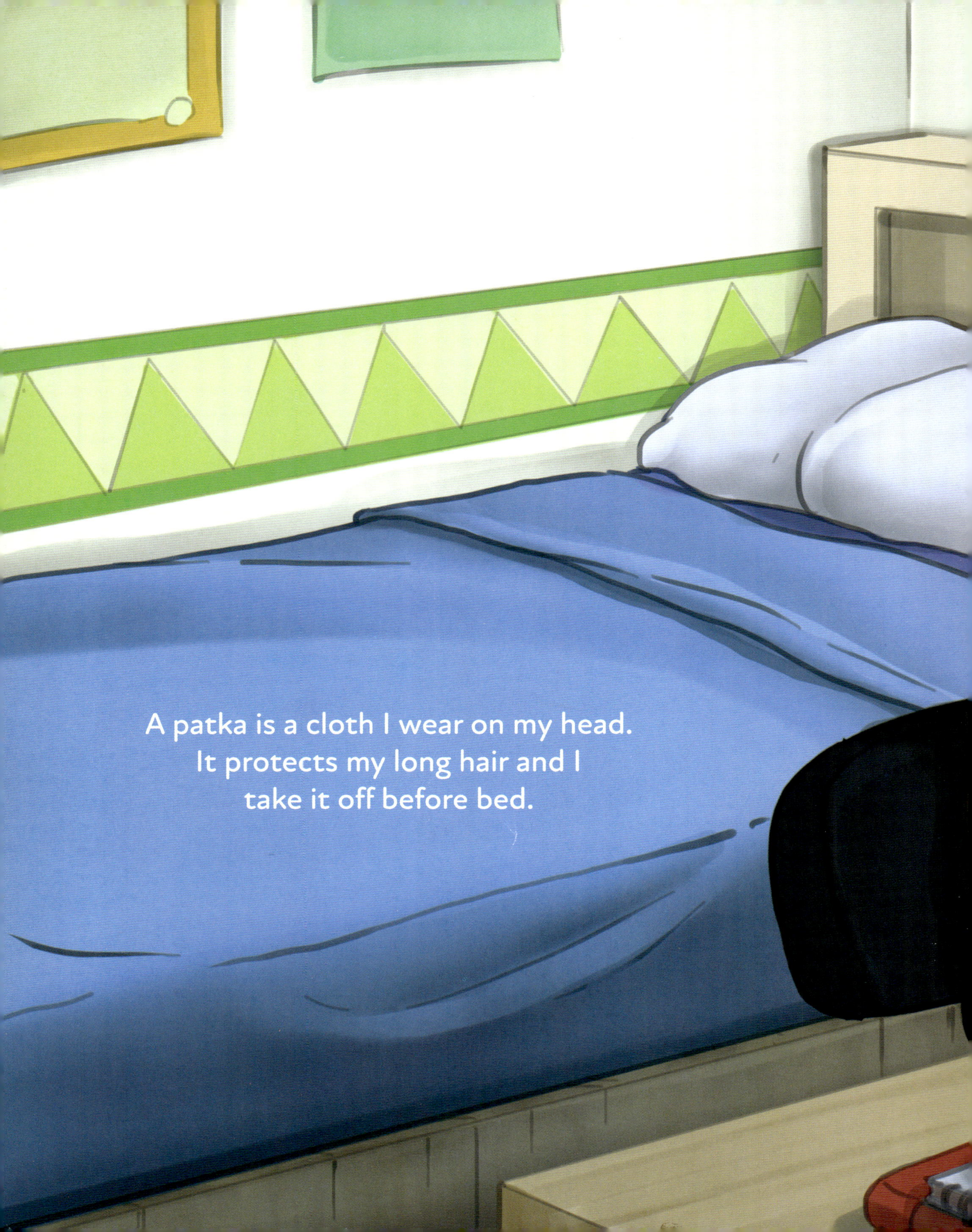

A patka is a cloth I wear on my head.
It protects my long hair and I
take it off before bed.

Being a Sikh means I am honest and do good when I can.
I work hard and always lend a helping hand.

On **Mondays,** I wear a patka that's **blue.**
I pretend I am a pilot. Do you like flying, too?

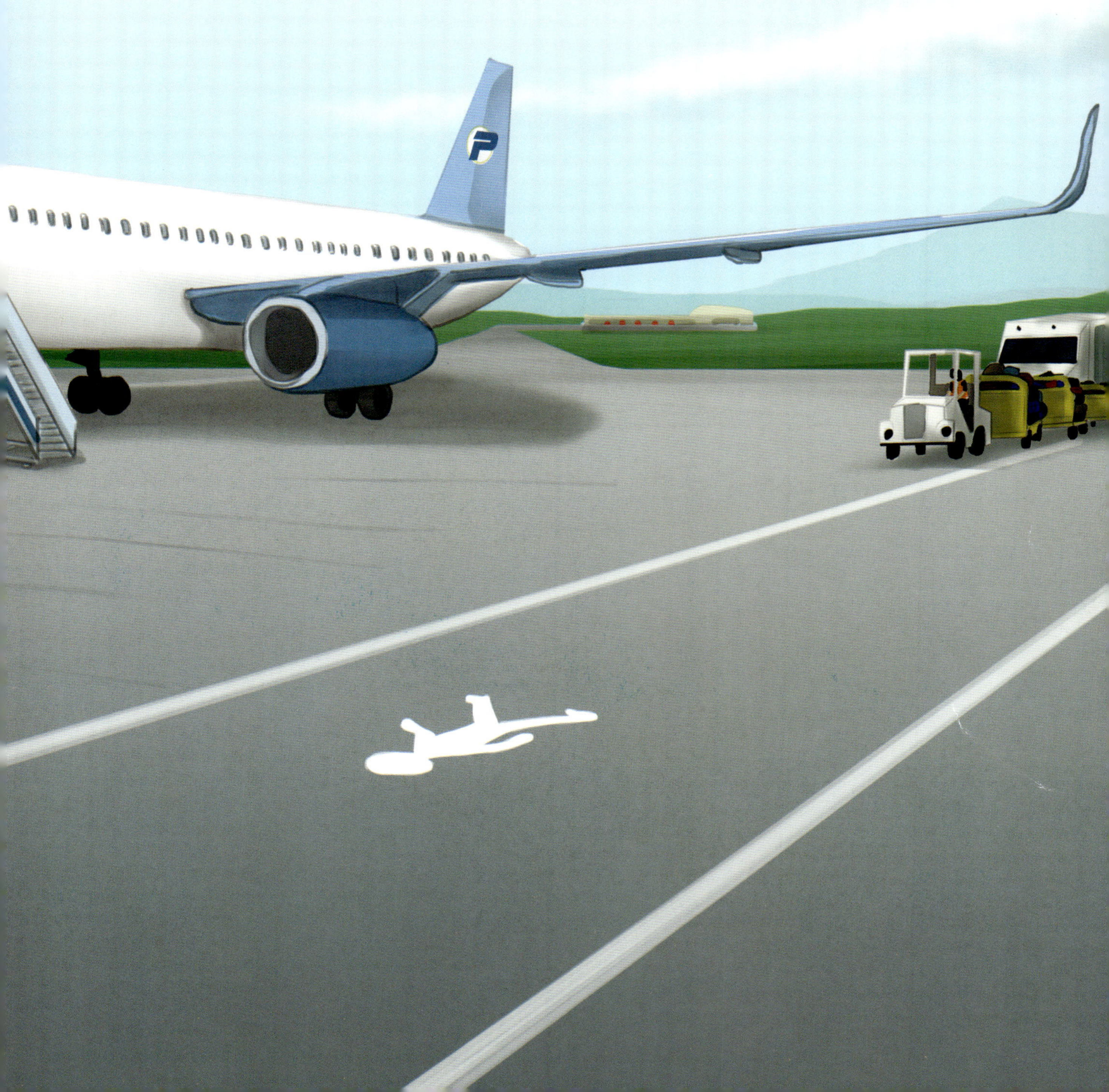

On **Tuesdays,** I wear a patka that's **red.**
I pretend I am a firefighter—
watch out ahead!

On **Wednesdays,** I wear a patka that's **black.**
I pretend I am a policeman keeping traffic on track.

On **Thursdays**, I wear a patka that's **green.**
I dress up in silly costumes and pretend it's Halloween.

On **Fridays**, I wear a patka that's **orange.**
I pretend I am a superhero saving the world with lots of courage.

On **Saturdays**, I wear a patka that's **yellow.**
I pretend I am a soccer player kicking and scoring a **GOOOOAL!**

On **Sundays**, I wear a patka that's **white.**
I pretend I am an astronaut ready to take flight.

Every day I wear a patka of any color that I choose.
It's a part of my outfit: patka, clothes, socks, and shoes!

2020 June
23
monday

My patka color lets me be whoever I want to be,
but best of all, when I wear it, I get to be ME!

Now, my friends, I must ask you this—
if *you* could choose a color, which would you pick?

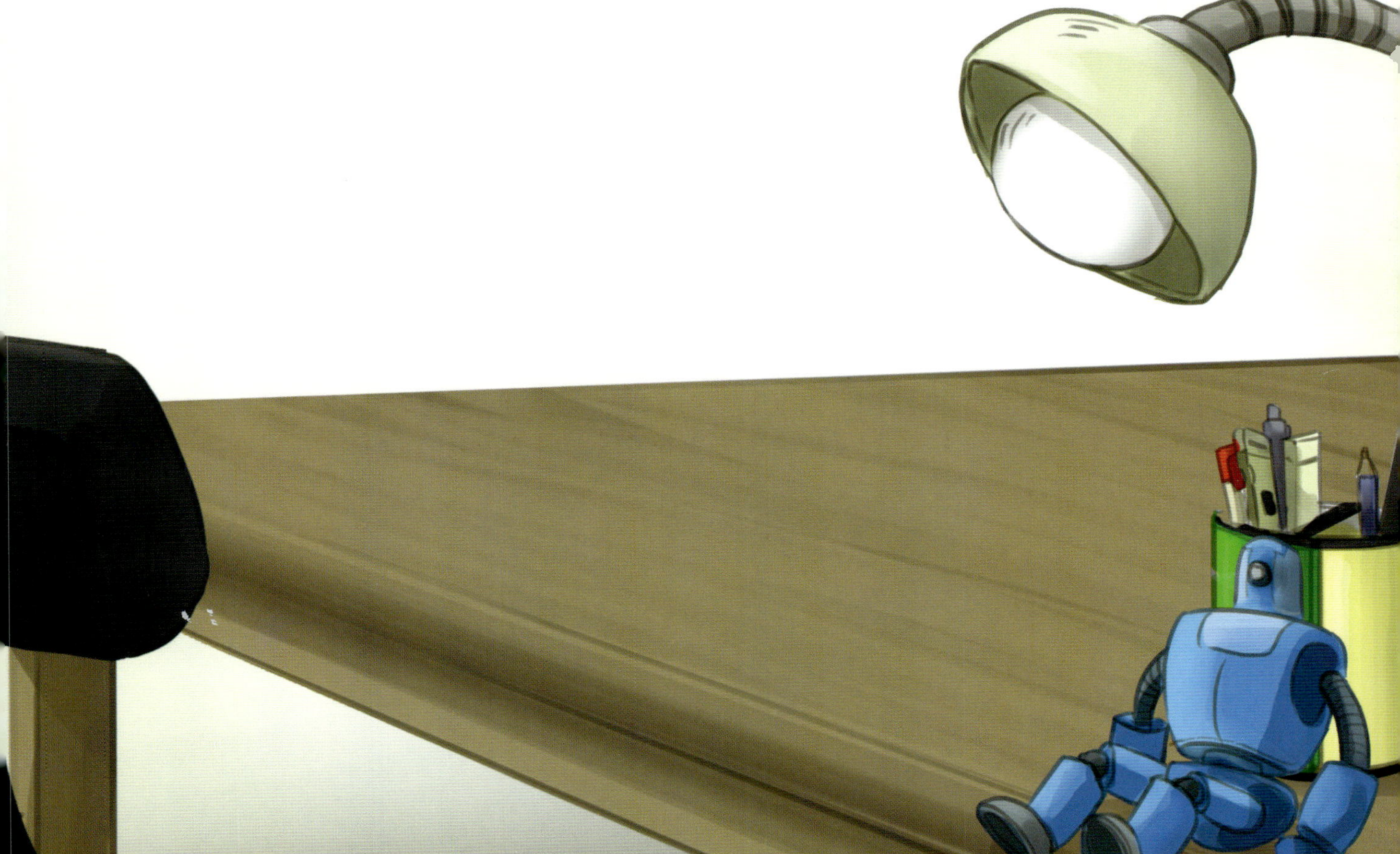

Sikhism Facts:

- Sikh, in Punjabi, means disciple or learner.
- Sikhism is the 5th largest religion, with over 30 million Sikhs worldwide.
- The Sikh turban and patka are symbols of humility, integrity, and discipline.
- Sikhism teaches that men and women of all races and religions are equal.

3 Core Beliefs:

1. Naam Japna (Always remember God)
2. Kirat Karni (Earn an honest living)
3. Vand Chakna (Share with everyone)

Deepika Kaur Pujji is a St. Louis native, wife, and mother of 2 beautiful children. After completing her psychology and advertising degree from Boston University, she spent time as a digital advertising professional at global ad agencies and Twitter. In 2015, she received the promotion of a lifetime to full-time Mama.